Welsh for Visitors

A Little goes a Long Way

Vítejte Aspádzomai Hoş geldiniz Degemer mat Üdvözlet Selamat datang
Sveiki Witamy Benvinguts Croeso Haere mai Benvinguts Sveiki
Bienvenidos Merħba Bem-vindos Bienvenue Aloha Haykuykuy! Добро
пожаловать! 欢迎 Willkommen Welcome Salve Fàilte
Velkommen Bine ati venit Hoşgeldiniz Benvido Wëllkomm

Elin Angharad Davies

D0227404

First published in 2018
© text: Elin Angharad Davies
© publication: Gwasg Carreg Gwalch 2018

ISBN: 978-1-84524-285-5

Cover design: Eleri Owen

Published by Gwasg Carreg Gwalch,
12 Iard yr Orsaf, Llanrwst, Wales LL26 0EH
tel: 01492 642031
email: books@carreg-gwalch.cymru
website: www.carreg-gwalch.cymru

Acknowledgements

General visitors' attractions:
© Images: Crown copyright (2018) Visit Wales

page 13: Welsh FA, Cymdeithas Bêl-droed Cymru
page 17: Lleol Cymru

Detailed signs etc.: Gwasg Carreg Gwalch

Cover image: Penrhyn Quarry Zip Wire
Image page 1: Above Siop y Pethe, Aberystwyth
Below: Bilingual architectural poetry by
Gwyneth Lewis, Millenium Centre Cardiff

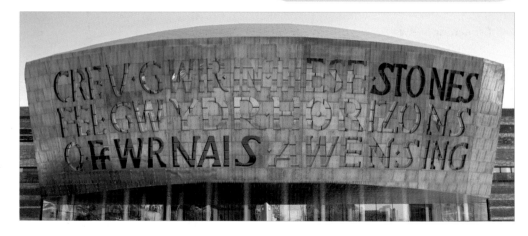

Cynnwys Contents

Language is so much more than words

In Early Welsh, **iaith** – the Welsh word for language – was also used for those who spoke that language, the people whom the language united together. It was therefore one of the first words in any culture for the concept of what we would now call a **nation**.

Welsh derives from a branch of the Celtic family of the Indo-European languages and is closely related to Cornish and Breton. The Welsh language is mostly Celtic but, like many other languages, has borrowed from languages such as Latin, Irish, Norse, Norman French and English.

The Welsh alphabet has 29 letters consisting of 22 consonants and 7 vowels (**a, e, i, o, u, w, y**). Welsh is a phonetic language. Once you know how to pronounce each individual letter you will be able to pronounce a word!

• The accent is almost always on the penultimate syllable.

• There is no indefinite article (a, an) in Welsh; nouns are either feminine or masculine.

• Adjectives follow nouns and numbers – an **orange bike** would be a **beic oren** in Welsh, a complete flip to the English.

• Welsh has a formal and informal way to address someone, as do most other languages, English being an exception. **Chi** is formal and **ti** is informal and both mean **you**. The first is used when talking to someone you've never met before or someone you respect, e.g. your boss, and the second is for close friends, family and children. **Chi** is also used when addressing a group of people – **you** (plural).

• Like many other languages there are standard and spoken forms in Welsh. Most Welsh courses for adults teach the spoken forms and concentrate on creating Welsh speakers.

In 1901, 50% of the Welsh population spoke Welsh but by 2011 that percentage had fallen to 19% due to an influx of English speakers moving into the country. In early 1962, Saunders Lewis delivered a radio speech called '*Tynged yr Iaith*' (The Fate of the Language) where he envisaged that Welsh as a spoken language would die if things were to carry on as they were. In reaction to this, Cymdeithas yr Iaith (*The Welsh Language*

the Commissioner to impose regulations on organisations.

There is strong support for the language among the vast majority of the population and more and more bilingual schools appear annually. The Welsh Government aims to increase the number of Welsh speakers to a total of one million by 2050. A National Centre for Learning Welsh has been established to manage the provision of Welsh courses for adults in Wales and there are 11 providers across Wales which deliver Welsh courses on the Centre's behalf. Want to give Welsh a go? www.learnwelsh.cymru

Opening parade at Llangollen International Eisteddfod

Society) emerged as a direct action pressure group campaigning for Welsh rights. They began by painting monolingual road signs with Cymdeithas symbols and Welsh place names.

Landmark victories were won by the language movement – Welsh is now an official language in Wales, with equal status. Under the 2011 Welsh Language Act, a Welsh Language Commissioner was appointed to promote and facilitate the use of the language, and to work towards ensuring that Welsh is treated no less favourably than English. In 2015, the Welsh Assembly passed the Welsh Language Standards that allow

A Welsh Duolingo course was created in 2018, and within a few weeks, a million students had signed up.

When we go to France or Italy, we try the local wine and venture a few words in their national languages. In Wales, the same applies: enjoy the country, feast on the scenery and the produce – and use a few words in Welsh. The warm Welsh **Croeso** will immediately rise a few degrees to acknowledge your efforts!

Tipyn Bach goes a Long Way

'Can you speak Welsh?' is a question often asked in Wales.

'Tipyn bach' (just a little) is very often the answer!

But **'just a little'** Cymraeg goes further than you might think! Just a few words, just an attempt to pronounce Welsh place names or a person's name, goes a long way. Showing an interest in a different language and culture gives a whole new aspect when visiting any country and is a big bonus when attempting to communicate and socialise.

Why not try
Helo with a Welsh accent, when you're greeting someone!
Follow that with a **Ti'n iawn? (You OK?)**
Say **diolch** when **thanking someone**
Give **os gwelwch yn dda** a go rather than saying **please**.
Say **Iechyd Da** instead of **Cheers!**

Every new language you delve into opens a window into a new world. You learn more about culture, heritage, history and the people when learning another language.

We hope you enjoy your trip to Wales and that you'll give Welsh a go!

At the start: Hanner Marathon Caerdydd,
Cardiff Half Marathon

★ *Top Ten Welsh Words:* **Croeso**

Croeso – Welcome
Croeso i Gymru! – Welcome to Wales!
Croeso can also be used as 'you're welcome' after you've heard **diolch** (thank you).

Croeso i Gymru! – Welcome to Wales! I'm sure you've seen this word before. We're a very welcoming country and some areas that are popular with visitors even have croeso signs as you enter the villages and towns: **Croeso i Aberystwyth**.

Croeso has long been a part of Welsh heritage and was very important in Cyfraith Hywel Dda (*Hywel Dda's Law* – the traditional Law Code of Wales laid down in the 9th century) where it was of great importance to look after and care for guests or visitors and grant them legal protection. **Bwrdd Croeso Cymru** the Welsh Tourist Board was established in 1969 but was replaced in 2006 by Visit Wales or in Cymraeg, **Croeso Cymru**. **Canolfannau Croeso** *(Welcome centres)* is the Welsh term for tourist information centres, of which there are around 35 in Wales. Every year, the tourist industry brings more than £5 billion into Wales, so **croeso** to you, and a very warm welcome it is too!

A **Croeso** *design at the entrance to the National Eisteddfod of Wales*

Bienvenue   Willkommen   Bienvenida   Benvenuto   Welkom   Witamy

Cymru – **Wales**
Cymru – **the country**
Cymry – **the people of Wales**
Cymro – **a Welshman**
Cymraes – **a Welshwoman**
Cymraeg – **Welsh (the language)**
Cymreig – **Welsh (adjective)**

Over 3 million people live in Wales and we have two official languages: **Cymraeg** and **Saesneg** (English). In 1997, Wales voted to devolve powers from London to the Senedd (Parliament) in Cardiff.

Wales has a long industrial history, mining for copper, slate, gold, iron and lead dating from the Roman era to a much larger scale in the 18th century. By 1850 **Cymru** was the first industrial country in the world, with more working in industry than in agriculture. The Welsh industries vastly contributed to the British Empire's wealth and power in her day, especially when the famous coal mines were in operation.

As **Cymru** moved further away from heavy industry, some historians state that it was this industrial past that kept the Welsh language alive. Although accidents were common and the cost of clearing the land after mine closures was high, these industries kept the Welsh people in Wales. This was true for the whole of Wales, and compared with other minority languages, Wales' industrial past may have played a big role in keeping the language alive.

The country's slogan is **'Cymru am byth'** (Wales for ever! / Long Live Wales!) – there are T-shirts and scarves for football and rugby fans, souvenirs and car stickers all proclaiming **Cymru am byth!** Our loyalty or faithfulness to our country is prominent in the national anthem, **Hen Wlad fy Nhadau** (The Land of my Fathers).

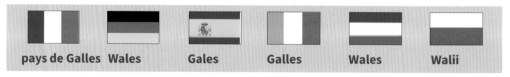

pays de Galles Wales Gales Galles Wales Walii

★ *Top Ten Welsh Words:* **Diolch**

Diolch – Thank you
Diolch yn fawr – Thank you very much
Llawer o ddiolch – Many thanks
Canmil diolch!
– a hundred thousand thanks!

During Euro 2016, the Welsh football team felt a great deal of support from the **Cymry** and even though they lost to Portugal in the semi-final the first thing on the players' minds was to thank the fans by wearing **diolch** T-shirts. The whole of Wales was behind the team and the 'Red Wall' of fans during every game was legendary. *'Allez Cymru'* was a popular French phrase, and many pub landlords thanked the Welsh for their good behaviour. One barman, Nicolas Zimmerman, said that the Welsh were now 'brothers' as it was always a 'good atmosphere' when the Welsh were around. The biggest **diolch** during Euro 2016 came was from the chief police officer in Bordeaux, when he thanked the Welsh fans for their good behaviour during a press conference.

Recently, Christmas and New Year was a very challenging time for the Welsh Blood Service. Wintry weather combined with colds and flu reduced blood stocks and there was a shortfall of 1,000 donations. The service made an urgent appeal and the support was 'truly amazing'. When blood stocks in Wales returned to a healthy level, the Welsh Blood Service wrote a **diolch** article on their website to thank everyone for donating and to remind them of how important their donations were to the Service: **Ni allwn gyflenwi ein hysbytai hebddoch CHI (We couldn't supply our hospitals without YOU!)**, ending with a **diolch unwaith eto (thank you once again)**.

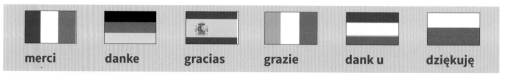

merci   **danke**   **gracias**   **grazie**   **dank u**   **dziękuję**

★ *Top Ten Welsh Words:* **Iechyd da!**

Iechyd da! – Cheers!

Iechyd da literally means **'good health'**. It is the Welsh national drinking toast – **Cheers!** It is seen on Welsh craft beer bottle labels and Welsh whiskey adverts.

It was inevitable that a brewery would call itself **Iechyd da! Cwrw** means **ale or beer** and Wales has over a hundred craft breweries, the most per capita in the world! This might well be the most important Welsh word to learn on your visit to **Cymru**! There is a real passion for local ales and spirits, especially when the breweries combine good taste with a taste of Welsh history. Cwrw Llŷn brewery combines local ales with local tales and legends whilst Cwrw Ogwen pays tribute to the history of Bethesda, its authors and industrial past. Funnily enough, the **Iechyd Da** brewery is based in Elkhart, Indiana in America!

Iechyd da, as well as being related to drinking, can also refer to keeping fit and healthy. Wales boasts a gym (Cardiff), deli (Betws-y-coed, Caernarfon and Llanymddyfri) and health food shop (Llanymddyfri) all christened **Iechyd Da**.

Since 2017, Members of Parliament are allowed to use their **Cymraeg** during meetings of the Welsh Affairs Committee, which has 40 members in parliament. Before then, the use of **Cymraeg** was banned in the houses of parliament in London. Members are now allowed to start their speech with the words '**Iechyd da...**'

A **Iechyd Da** *brewery glass*

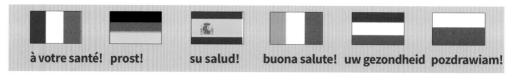

à votre santé!   **prost!**   **su salud!**   **buona salute!**   **uw gezondheid**   **pozdrawiam!**

Modryb Elin Ennog,
os gwelwch chi'n dda, ga i grempog?
Cewch chithau de a siwgr gwyn,
a phwdin lond eich ffedog.

Aunty Elin Ennog,
please can I have a pancake?
you may have tea and white sugar,
and an apron full of pudding.

Os gwelwch yn dda – Please

What's the magic word? We even have a nursery rhyme **(hwiangerdd)** that reminds children to ask politely, **os gwelwch chi'n dda ga i grempog?**

It looks like a really long word for a please, right? It's the same as the French, **si il vous plaît** which literally means **'if it pleases you'** and **os gwelwch yn dda** literally means **'if you see fit / well'**.

If you can't remember the long-winded way of saying please in Welsh, there's always a get-out clause... say please with a Welsh accent: **plîs!**

Happy Pancake Day

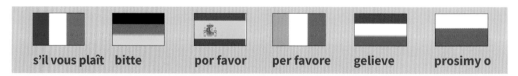

s'il vous plaît   bitte   por favor   per favore   gelieve   prosimy o

Dydd Crempog Hapus

★ *Top Ten Welsh Words:* **Hwyl!**

Hwyl! – Goodbye!

As with greeting, saying **goodbye** in Welsh goes a long way.

Hwyl literally means a **sail**, and wishing sailors a **hwyl fawr (big sail)** as they were leaving dry land meant that you were saying goodbye and also wishing them a safe journey home.

Like a lot of words in Cymraeg, **hwyl** has another meaning, **fun**:
Lot o hwyl – lots of fun

We also refer to **hwyl** when we talk about mood, **sut hwyl? – how are you / how's your mood?** Denmark has *hygge*, but Wales has **hwyl**, the idea of mood and emotion. We can say that someone has **mynd i hwyl** if a speaker has suddenly felt passionate about something and is carried away by emotion or if someone suddenly sings from the heart, especially when the songs are hymns or rugby chants. The Welsh Rugby team can **mynd i hwyl** on the rugby field and again, this implies that they have passion and spirit.

Ar frig y don
On the crest of the wave

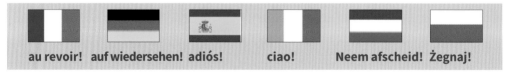

au revoir!   auf wiedersehen!   adiós!   ciao!   Neem afscheid!   Żegnaj!

★ Top Ten Welsh Words: **Tŷ**

Tŷ – House

We have a lot of famous houses in Cymru. Have you heard of the **Tŷ Coch** in Porth Dinllaen (Llŷn)? It's the third best beach bar in the world and serves local beers, ales and spirits – **coch** is **red**, denoting that it is built of bricks. **Tŷ Hyll (the ugly house or the rugged house – bottom right opposite)** is the Snowdonia Society's flagship property located near Betws-y-coed which offers nature and conservation activities. Here you will find a tearoom and a wildlife garden. **Tŷ Mawr Wybrnant**, a National Trust property located in Penmachno near Betws-y-coed is the birthplace of Bishop William Morgan, the first translator of the Bible into Cymraeg. **Tŷ Siamas** in Dolgellau is named in memory of Elis Siôn Siamas, a famous harpist from Llanfachreth, near Dolgellau in Meirionnydd. It was built around 1870 and now houses a shop, cafe, bar, performing auditorium and recording studio.

A pub can be called a tafarn or **tŷ tafarn (public house)** and a **toilet** is **tŷ bach** (literally a **little house** – usually at the bottom of the garden)! A restaurant is **bwyty (bwyd + tŷ)** literally meaning a **food house** and cows don't sleep in a cow-shed in Wales, they sleep in a **beudy (beu + tŷ)** or **cow-house**!

You might also hear:

Adref   homewards, home
Cartref home (the building)

Many famous and renowned Welsh people were born and bred in houses, rather than castles or palaces – they were workers rather than royalty. **Tŷ** therefore refers to family, home and culture.

Tŷ Coch **on the beach at Porth Dinllaen**
Tŷ Hafan **children's hospice charity shop**
Tŷ Hyll **the rugged house of Snowdonia**

| maison | haus | casa | azienda | huis | dom |

★ *Top Ten Welsh Words:* **Un**

Un – One

The Welsh counting system is classically European. Like other ancient cultures, such as Latin and Basque, counting in fives and tens is fundamental, as that's how many fingers you have on each hand! Moving on to more complex numbers, we can use the old-fashioned 'twenty' system (**un ar ddeg** – **one on ten**) or the more modern system (**un deg un** – **one ten one**). The twenty system was often used for trade, and interestingly, the Basque word for 20 is very similar to the Welsh **ugain**. One theory is that this similarity is evidence of the old trade paths on the north European shores where the Celts and Basques frequently traded.

The saying, **un bob un** – **one for each one** is rooted in our culture and means more than just clinching a deal in mathematical terms. It's about fairness and equality.

In the old Welsh laws, every son was treated equally and given an equal share of the father's land. This was very different to the principles of the Saxons and the Normans, whereby everything was given to the first-born son.

When a number of **Cymry** decided to emigrate to Patagonia in 1865 to create a new and better life for themselves and their families, the idea of one vote per individual was quickly grasped. This was the first state in the history of the world to give men and women an equal right to vote.

*Cymru'n Un – Wales united **is used in coalition politics from time to time. It originates from a union between the Welsh Princes under the leadership of Owain Gwynedd in 1165 which resisted Henry II's attempt to conquer the country. Henry's army was defeated in the battle of Crogen that very year.***

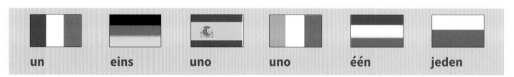

| un | eins | uno | uno | één | jeden |

MAE'R PLAC HWN I GOFFÁU • THIS PLAQUE COMMEMORATES

THIS BATTLE WAS PART
OF THE BERWYN MOUNTAINS
CAMPAIGN AS WALES FOUGHT FOR ITS
FREEDOM FROM ENGLISH DOMINATION

OWAIN GWYNEDD GRUFFUDD MAELOR HENRY II

THE BATTLE OF CROGEN

YMA' ROEDD BRWYDR CROGEN RHWNG BYDDIN
HENRI II BRENIN LLOEGR A BYDDIN CYMRU DAN
ARWEINIAD OWAIN GWYNEDD
NEARBY IN AUGUST 1165 A BLOODY BATTLE WAS FOUGHT
BETWEEN HENRY II, KING OF ENGLAND (r.1154–89) AND
WELSH FORCES UNDER OWAIN GWYNEDD (1137–70)

PLAQUE INITIATED BY DERYN POPPITT & MARK WILLIAMS
FUNDED BY CADBURY'S, CHIRK AND UNVEILED BY
COUNCILLOR ALED ROBERTS, LEADER, WREXHAM
COUNTY BOROUGH COUNCIL
4 MARCH 2009

OWAIN GWYNEDD • GRUFFUDD MAELOR • LORD RHYS • IORWERTH GOCH • OWAIN CYFEILIOG • EINION CLUD

★ Top Ten Welsh Words: **Dau**

Dau – Two

Un and **un** creates a pair. What can we say about the courtship rituals of the Welsh? Santes Dwynwen is the Welsh patron saint of lovers. She is celebrated throughout Wales on the 25th January and is connected with Ynys Llanddwyn, an island off the western coast of Anglesey. Even though Dwynwen is our patron saint of love, her love story was a tragic one. Dwynwen fell in love with Maelon, who asked her father for her hand in marriage. The request was refused and Dwynwen was told to find another suitor. But if Dwynwen couldn't have Maelon then she didn't want anyone else to have him. She met an angel and was given a potion. She gave this potion to Maelon and instantly he was turned into a block of ice. Dwynwen, rife with guilt, prayed for three requests: that Maelon be released, that she should never marry, and that God would guard all lovers.

The Welsh are famous for their love spoons. A love spoon was usually given to a young woman by her suitor. It was important for the young woman's father to see that the suitor was capable of providing for the family, and he would be judged by his woodwork. Sailors would often carve love spoons during their long journeys, which is why anchors would often be incorporated into carvings. Certain symbols came to have specific meanings: a horseshoe for luck, a cross for faith, hearts for love, a lock for security and a caged ball indicated the number of children hoped for. Love spoons are still produced and given as gifts on special occasions.

*Dau gariad – **for two lovers, what better gift than a Welsh love spoon?***

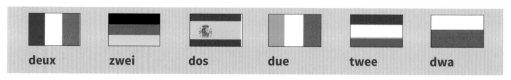

deux   zwei   dos   due   twee   dwa

Tri – Three

The idea that the number three is lucky is rooted deep in many cultures. In Wales, one of the most popular sayings when things haven't quite gone our way is **Tri chynnig i Gymro – three attempts for a Welshman / Third time lucky**. In Christianity, the number three represents the Holy Trinity and the three wise men, and fate smiles on anything associated with the number three. Three is also a lucky number in Chinese tradition. In 2014 a man in Beijing paid $215,000 for the lucky mobile number, 133-3333-3333. It is believed in Chinese culture that groups of three are even luckier. A Chinese proverb states that 'The wisdom of three ordinary people exceeds that of the wisest individual.'

In Welsh churches, preachers would include three sections to their sermons. They thought that it would be easier for an audience to remember their message if it was presented in threes. In Welsh tradition there are medieval transcripts that include **Trioedd Ynys Prydain – The Triads of the Island of Britain**. They are based on an extremely old oral memory and include lists of kings, heroes and villains, all in threes: sort of handbook to the traditional history of the Welsh.

In Welsh poetry, rhyming every three lines, and also three-line verses, have been a very important part of the bardic tradition for over a thousand years. A famous Welsh poem by the bard Aneirin, *Y Gododdin*, portrays a heroic army of 300 **(tri chant)** Welsh soldiers who met an army of ten thousand at the battle of Catraeth and fought on until there was only one man left standing.

In Wales, standing stones are sometimes found in groups of three together – like this group at Llanfechell, Anglesey

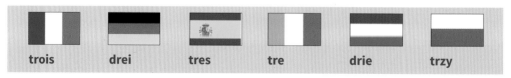

| trois | drei | tres | tre | drie | trzy |

★ Pronounciation

There are 29 letters in the Welsh alphabet, 22 consonants and 7 vowels.

The Welsh language is very phonetic and once you know how to pronounce the letters the sound rarely changes. If you can handle these sentences in English then you will have no trouble giving **Cymraeg** a go:

the tip had to refuse refuse.
he decided to desert the dessert in the desert.
the dove dove into the bushes.

What are you waiting for?

Phonetic

a	c**a**r/c**a**t
b	**b**ad
c	**k**ing
ch	Lo**ch**
d	**d**oor
dd	**th**is/**th**at
e	**a**ir/**e**gg
f	**v**iolin
ff	o**ff**
g	**g**ood
ng	ga**ng**
h	**h**ook
i	tr**ee**/**i**nk
j	**j**am
l	**l**and
ll	**l**and (+blow)
m	**m**ud
n	**n**orth
o	r**oa**r/**o**range
p	**p**iano
ph	**ph**ysics
r	**r**ed (+roll)
rh	**r**ed (+blow)
s	**s**tar
t	**t**ank
th	**th**in
u	b**ee**n/**ti**n
w	l**oo**k/**w**ater/c**oo**l
y	*'**uh**'/b**ee**n

* **y** changes depending on its location in a word.

y is an '**uh**' sound except when it's located in the last syllable, it then takes on an '**i**' sound:
mynydd (mountain) m**uh**nith
Talyllyn Tal-**uh**-llin

Talyllyn Railway

Dw i I am

Want to introduce yourself in Welsh? Just say…

I'm Siôn **Siôn dw i**

In **Cymraeg** we are literally saying 'Siôn I am' like in the ditty 'Henry the VIII I am, I am', it's exactly the same pattern in Welsh when we introduce ourselves.

If we want to say what we do, we follow the exact same pattern, replacing our name with our job title:

Nyrs dw i   I'm a nurse
Doctor dw i   I'm a doctor

If you want to say that you like something, **dw i** then needs to be moved to the very beginning of your sentence followed by **licio** or **hoffi**:

I like …   Dw i'n licio …
             Dw i'n hoffi …

Dw i'n licio golff   I like golf
Dw i'n hoffi ioga   I like yoga
Dw i'n licio siarad Cymraeg
I like speaking Welsh

Try this!
Dw i'n licio gwin gwyn sych!*
I like dry white wine!
Dw i'n hoffi cwrw tywyll!*
I like dark beer!
Dwi'n hoffi coffi!
I like coffee!

*remember the **'ch'** at the end of **sych** ('ch' like in lo**ch** not **ch**ocolate or **ch**allenge)
the **'ll' sound is created by pushing your tongue behind your teeth and blowing out through the side gaps or by just doing your finest impression of an angry cat! Go for it!

You might even want to try
Dw i'n dysgu Cymraeg
I'm learning Welsh

Do you like white water?
Ydw, dw i'n licio dŵr gwyllt!

A simple naming of what you want and adding **os gwelwch yn dda** is acceptable, exactly the same as you would do in English: **coffi, os gwelwch yn dda**
coffee, please

Yn y bar
peint, os gwelwch yn dda
a pint, please
gwin, os gwelwch yn dda
wine, please

You can also add some specifics
gwin gwyn mawr, os gwelwch yn dda
a large white wine please
gwin coch bach, os gwelwch yn dda
a small red wine, please
wisgi dwbl, os gwelwch yn dda
a double whiskey, please

Yn y caffi
*****cacen, os gwelwch yn dda**
a cake, please
******cacenni cri, os gwelwch yn dda**
Welsh cakes, please
te, os gwelwch yn dda
tea, please

*****panad o de, os gwelwch yn dda**
a cuppa tea, please
panad o goffi, os gwelwch yn dda
a cuppa coffee, please
dŵr, os gwelwch yn dda
water, please

*you might also hear **teisen** for cake
there are many names for Welsh cakes yn Gymraeg: **pice bach, pice ar y maen, cacenni cri
***you might also hear **disgled o de** for a cup of tea.

Just as with ordering food and drink, a simple naming of what you want and adding **os gwelwch yn dda** is acceptable when visiting a shop:
papur, os gwelwch yn dda
a paper, please
Want to ask how much something is?
Faint*, os gwelwch yn dda?

*Remember that an **f** is always a **v** sound **yn Gymraeg**, you are not commanding someone to swoon, just asking how much something costs!

Lle   Where
Ble

Want to ask where somewhere or someone is yn Gymraeg? Just say…

Lle mae …?   **Where is … ?**
Ble mae …?

Lle mae Ffordd Aberystwyth?
Where's Aberystwyth Road?

Ble mae John?
Where's John?

Lle (= place) and **Ble** (= what place) are completely interchangable in this setting.

If it's somewhere more specific, ask,

Lle mae'r … ?   **Where is the … ?**
Ble mae'r … ?

Lle mae'r tŷ bach?
Where's the toilet?
Ble mae'r gwesty?
Where's the hotel?
Lle mae'r caffi?
Where's the café?
Ble mae'r dafarn?
Where's the pub?
Lle mae'r maes parcio?
Where's the car park?
Ble mae'r traeth?
Where's the beach?
Lle mae'r ŵyl?
Where's the festival?

(from top, left to right)
Hay Literary Festival
and the Green Man Festival

★ Easy Welsh 4

Dim No/Not/None

A very handy negative word which offers phrases that covers many occasions:

Not that one	**Dim hwnna**
None left	**Dim ar ôl**
No thank you	**Dim diolch**

Here are a few that you should take heed of:

Dim Parcio	**No Parking**
Dim Mynediad	**No Entry**
Dim Nofio	**No Swimming**

Other everyday usage:

Dim ar gael	**Not available**
Dim amser	**No time**
Dim rŵan / Dim nawr	**Not now**
Dim o gwbwl	**Not at all**
Dim ysmygu	**No smoking**

As in many other languages, this phrase has a range of meanings:

Dim problem	**No problem / Don't mention it**

When you thank a waiter, or appreciate any kind of help or service, you will often hear **Dim problem!** meaning **Croeso! (You're welcome / Don't mention it)**. This is in general use in many languages of course: No problemo!

The word **problem** possibly arrived in Wales with the Romans, whose **problema** in turn was borrowed from the Greeks. There is an old story about a Roman official who turned to an Old Welsh leader to thank him for his kindness and was surprised to hear him answer with **Dim problem!**

'Yours is a funny language!' said the Roman, 'you haven't got your own word for **problem**!'

'Listen,' said the native, 'until the Romans arrived, we didn't have a problem.'

DIM LLYGAID CATHOD
NO CATS EYES

m Ysbwriel

Dim Beicio

No Litter

No Cycling

Dim o gwbl
At any time

★ Handy phrases

When meeting

helo	hello
ti'n iawn?	you OK?
shwmae? / su'mae?	how are you?
bore da	good morning
p'nawn da	good afternoon
noswaith dda*	good evening

*Noswaith dda** is only used in formal situations. Avoid greeting everyone at the bar with this, a simple **helo** or a **su'mae / shwmae** is sufficient, or avoid it completely by visiting the pub earlier on in the day...!

When leaving

hwyl	good bye
ta ra	good bye
wela i chi	see you
nos da	good night

When you want to ask

lle mae'r ... ?	where is the ... ?
faint, os gwelwch yn dda?	
how much, please?	

When you're stuck

help!	help!
esgusodwch fi	excuse me
dw i ddim yn deall	I don't understand
dw i ddim yn gwybod	I don't know
dw i ddim yn siŵr	I'm not sure
Beth ydy ... yn Gymraeg?	
What is ... in Welsh?	
Beth ydy ... yn Saesneg?	
What is ... in English?	

Bore da. Faint os gwelwch yn dda?
Good morning. How much please?

★ Greetings

Helo – Hello
Looks the same doesn't it? Just say it with a Welsh accent!

Shwmae? Su'mae? – How are you?
Cymraeg has different dialects, just like any other language. There are some differences between the Welsh you'll hear in the north and the south and **Shwmae / Su'mae** conveys this subtle difference beautifully.

Diwrnod Shwmae Su'mae is held on the 15th of October. On this day we encourage everyone to give Welsh a go, and some establishments even reward their customers for using their Cymraeg!
   The first greeting is really important; it goes such a long way if you can start a conversation in Welsh, even if it is just a Helo with a Welsh accent!

Another common way of greeting someone is by asking **Ti'n iawn? – You OK?** – just the same as you would in English. This greeting is often followed by **iawn! – OK**.
['iawn' rhymes with the English 'town']

Other ways to say **Helo**:

Bore da – Good morning
Pnawn da – Good afternoon

*A Diwrnod Shwmae Su'mae **poster***

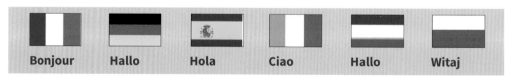

Bonjour   Hallo   Hola   Ciao   Hallo   Witaj

★ Crunching a few numbers

As easy as 1 – 2 – 3

0	dim
1	un
2	dau
3	tri
4	pedwar
5	pump
6	chwech
7	saith
8	wyth
9	naw
10	deg

Follow the same pattern

30	tri deg
40	pedwar deg
50	pum deg
60	chwe deg
70	saith deg
80	wyth deg
90	naw deg
100	cant

Still counting ...

11	un deg un
12	un deg dau
13	un deg tri
14	un deg pedwar
15	un deg pump
16	un deg chwech
17	un deg saith
18	un deg wyth
19	un deg naw
20	dau ddeg

(from top, left to right)
Un ar y mynydd, One on the mountain
Dau ar wyliau yn Aberaeron,
Two on holiday at Aberaeron
Cannoedd o sêr, Hundreds of stars

★ What is the time?

Faint o'r gloch ydy hi?
What time is it?

Mae'n chwech o'r gloch	06:00
Mae'n chwarter wedi chwech	06:15
Mae'n hanner awr wedi chwech	06:30
Mae'n chwarter i saith	06:45

... o'r gloch   ... o'clock
e.g.
un o'r gloch   one o'clock

chwarter wedi ...
quarter past ...
hanner awr wedi ...
half past ...
chwarter i ...
quarter to ...
Mae'n ...
It's ...

Mae'n amser brecwast
It's breakfast time
Mae'n amser cinio
It's lunch-time
Mae'n amser swper
It's supper-time

(from top, left to right)
Cloc tref Harlech, Harlech town clock
Cloc castell Caerdydd, Cardiff castle clock
Cloc marchnad Caerdydd, Cardiff Market clock

★ What's the weather like?

We all like to complain about the weather; it's either too hot or too cold, too breezy or not enough breeze or just plain damp and miserable. Now, you will be able to talk about the weather **yn Gymraeg**! Give these a go…

Mae'n braf   It's fine

Mae'n heulog   It's sunny

Mae'n gynnes It's warm

Mae'n boeth It's hot

Mae'n niwlog It's misty

Mae'n gymylog It's cloudy

Mae'n wyntog   It's windy

Mae'n wlyb   It's wet

Mae'n dawel   It's calm

Mae'n bwrw glaw!   It's raining!

Mae'n oer It's cold

Mae'n sych It's dry

Mae'n nosi It's dusk

Mae'n stormus It's stormy

Dyddiau'r wythnos
Days of the week

Dydd Llun	Monday
Nos Lun	Monday night
Dydd Mawrth	Tuesday
Nos Fawrth	Tuesday night
Dydd Mercher	Wednesday
Nos Fercher	Wednesday night
Dydd Iau	Thursday
Nos Iau	Thursday night
Dydd Gwener	Friday
Nos Wener	Friday night
Dydd Sadwrn	Saturday
Nos Sadwrn	Saturday night
Dydd Sul	Sunday
Nos Sul	Sunday night

Dydd Llun ydy hi
It's Monday
Dydd Mercher ydy hi
It's Wednesday
Nos Sadwrn ydy hi
It's Saturday night

An emoji mug with the days of the week:
Facebook: Dewi Wyn Ffotograffydd/Photographer
ETSY: DewiWynPwllheli

DYDD LLUN 😭
DYDD MAWRTH 😒
DYDD MERCHER 😬
DYDD IAU 😌
DYDD GWENER 😍
DYDD SADWRN 😜
DYDD SUL 😖

Misoedd Months

Ionawr	January
Chwefror	February
Mawrth	March
Ebrill	April
Mai	May
Mehefin	June
Gorffennaf	July
Awst	August
Medi	September
Hydref	October
Tachwedd	November
Rhagfyr	December

Tymhorau Seasons

y gwanwyn	spring
yr haf	summer
yr hydref	autumn
y gaeaf	winter

(from top, left to right)
*Gaeaf **Winter** Eryri **Snowdonia***
*Haf **Summer** Am dro yn y wlad **A walk in the country***
*Machlud **Sunset** Bae Caerdydd **Cardiff Bay***

Colours

Lliwiau Colours

coch	red
melyn	yellow
gwyrdd	green
glas	blue
porffor / piws	purple
oren	orange
brown	brown
pinc	pink
llwyd	grey
gwyn	white
du	black

When we describe things in **Cymraeg** the describing word comes second, therefore a **blue car** would be **car glas**, a **red house** would be **tŷ coch** and an **orange bike** would be **beic oren**.

If you want to ask what colour something is, try

Pa liw ydy'r ...   What colour is the ...
Pa liw ydy'r car? What colour is the car?
Pa liw ydy'r beic? What colour is the bike?
Pa liw ydy'r tŷ?   What colour is the house?

Want to know how to answer – just name the colour!

glas   oren   coch

If you want to describe the colour you can try

golau	light
tywyll	dark
llachar	bright

car glas golau   a light blue car
beic coch tywyll a dark red bike

(from top, left to right)
Ceremonial red dragon (Draig Goch) at the National Eisteddfod
Colourful beach huts at Llanbedrog
Welsh Black Cattle (Gwartheg Duon Cymreig) at the National Welsh Show

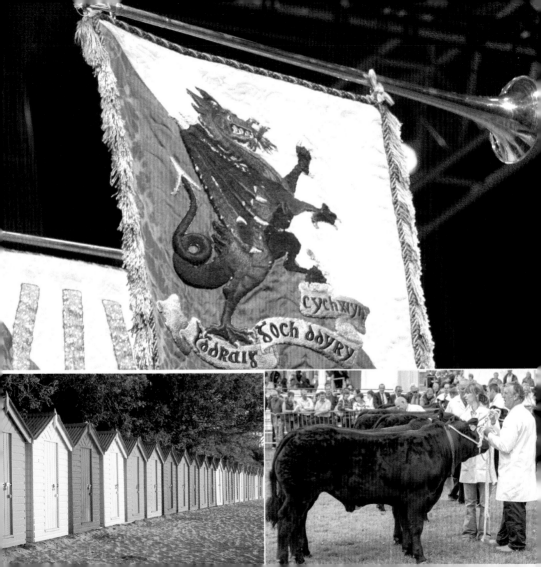

★ Travelling – by car

You might have noticed that there are bilingual road signs in **Cymru**. In 1972 the Bowen Committee recommended that all road signs in Cymru should be bilingual after protests from Cymdeithas yr Iaith.

Look out for…

safle bws	**bus stop**
maes parcio	**car park**
dim parcio	**no parking**
tocyn parcio	**parking ticket**
talu yma	**pay here**
gyrrwch yn ofalus	**drive safely**
ildiwch	**give way**
araf	**slow**
unffordd	**one way**
arafwch nawr	**reduce speed now**
allan	**out**

You might need to ask for directions…

Esgusodwch fi
Excuse me

Lle mae'r maes parcio?
Where's the car park?
Lle mae'r garej nesaf?
Where's the next garage?
Lle mae'r Stryd Fawr?
Where's the High Street?
Lle mae'r toiledau?
Where are the toilets?

★ Travelling – by rail

Tramways already existed in Welsh quarries, coal pits and ironworks before 1800, with the wagons pulled along by ponies or donkeys, or even women and children. But in 1804 the first steam engine pulled its load down the line, a sight seen for the first time in the world here in **Cymru** at the Penydarren ironworks in Merthyr Tydfil, where Richard Trevithick was an engineer.

Pryd mae'r trên nesaf?
When's the next train?
Pryd mae trên Bangor yn cyrraedd?
When does the Bangor train arrive?

Lle mae platfform un?
Where's platfform one?
Lle mae'r swyddfa docynnau?
Where's the ticket office?

Sedd wag?
Empty seat?

Try and pronounce the place names as you travel through **Cymru**. Want to understand the meaning of some place names? Take a look at these:

ffordd / lôn	**road / way**
aber	**estuary / mouth of the river**
llan	**the church of...**
stryd	**street**
caer	**fort**
dyffryn / cwm	**valley**
tref	**town**
dinas	**city**
pentref	**village**
glan	**river bank / shore**
llyn	**lake**
rhyd	**ford**
afon	**river**
mynydd	**mountain**
bryn	**hill**
ynys	**island**
nant	**stream**

(from top, left to right)
Northern coast train passing Conwy castle
Cambrian coast line
Minffordd station on Ffestiniog Railway

★ Travelling – by ferry

Because Wales has 750 miles of coastline, the sea has been a key element in the country's history. The first people to settle here came by sea and maritime connections were an essential part of early commerce, Celtic craft and culture and the spread of the Celtic church.

Later, ocean-going ships were important in Wales' industrial development: coal and slate, copper and granite were exported to Europe, with some ships travelling as far as America and Australia. The coal ports of Glamorgan and Gwent were the largest in the world.

Smaller vessels plied their trade between small ports, landing sometimes on sandy beaches, without a quay or harbour. These can be traced along the Welsh coast today as many beaches and coves are called **Porth... (port/entrance)** and the maritime heritage is very much an attractive part of a visit to Porth-gain, Porth Dinllaen and many other similar old ports.

The main ferry ports in Wales today are the western ports for Ireland: **Caergybi Holyhead** and **Abergwaun Fishguard**.

Pryd mae'r fferi yn gadael?
When does the ferry leave?

(from top, left to right)
The ferry from Ireland at Fishguard

★ Travelling – by air

Another 'first' is that it was Bill Frost, a village carpenter in Saundersfoot, Pembrokeshire, who built and flew the first aeroplane in 1896. He was the first man to fly, quite a few years earlier than the Wright brothers' flight in 1903.

There are two **airports** (**maes awyr**) in Cymru, one in **Caerdydd Cardiff** and the other at Y Fali, **Ynys Môn Anglesey**. **Maes Awyr y Fali** offers flights to **Caerdydd** twice a day, Monday to Friday, whilst Caerdydd offers a variety of destinations.

Pryd mae'r awyren yn gadael?
When does the aeroplane leave?

Air Wales
and Ambiwlans Awyr Cymru (Wales Air Ambilance)
– a charity used often to help visitors in Wales

★ Accommodation – hotels and guest houses

Ask for

Pris ystafell sengl, os gwelwch yn dda?
Price of a single room, please?

ystafell sengl	**single room**
ystafell twin	**twin room**
ystafell ddwbl	**double room**
ystafell deulu	**family room**

Dwy noson, os gwelwch yn dda
Two nights, please

noson	**one night**
dwy noson	**two nights**
tair noson	**three nights**
pedair noson	**four nights**
pum noson	**five nights**
chwe noson	**six nights**
wythnos	**a week**
pythefnos	**a fortnight**

Look out for

un seren	**one star**
dwy seren	**two stars**
tair seren	**three stars**
pedair seren	**four stars**
pum seren	**five stars**

In Welsh we have different genders for different nouns. When a noun is female, we use **dwy, tair, pedair** for 2, 3, 4.

(from top, left to right)
Llandudno promenade hotels;
Cricieth guest houses

★ Accommodation – camping and caravanning

Lle mae'r maes gwersylla?	where is the camp site?
Lle mae'r toiledau? / tŷ bach?	where are the toilets?
Lle mae'r siop agosaf?	where is the nearest shop?
Lle mae'r dafarn agosaf?	where is the nearest pub?

You might see

maes carafanau a phebyll	caravan and camping site
trydan	electricity (hook-up)
pabell / tent	a tent
carafanau teithiol	mobile homes
safleoedd tymhorol	seasonal pitches
dim tanau ar y gwellt	no campfires allowed
cŵn ar dennyn	dogs on a leash
dim cŵn	no dogs
ar agor	open
ar gael	available
toiledau / tai bach	toilets
cawod	shower

(from top, left to right)
Camping on the Gower peninsula
A glamping pod on Anglesey
Caravanning at Llanystumdwy

llety hunan-arlwyo	**self-catering accommodation**
bwthyn	**cottage**
bythynnod	**cottages**
tŷ	**house**
fflat	**flat**

un ystafell wely	**one bedroom**
dwy ystafell wely	**two bedroom**
tair ystafell wely	**three bedroom**
pedair ystafell wely	**four bedroom**
pum ystafell wely	**five bedroom**

When booking or on arrival, ask

Oes 'na wi-fi?	**Is there wi-fi?**
Oes 'na dân agored?	**Is there an open fire?**
Oes 'na siop yn agos?	**Is there a shop nearby?**
Oes 'na dafarn yn agos?	**Is there a pub nearby?**
Oes 'na fwyty yn agos?	**Is there a restaurant nearby?**

(from top, left to right)
Some of the fascinating accommodation at Portmeirion
Welsh deli produce

★ What's to see? – Castles

Castell Castle

There are many castles in Wales but only 49 are owned by Cadw, the Welsh Government's historic environment body / agency. **Cadw** means **to keep**. The first Welsh castles were built by the Normans to invade Welsh land from their strongholds in the Welsh Marches. The word 'castle / castell' was brought here by the Normans.

The Welsh kings and princes sharply built their own fortified castles – these can usually be found in the valleys and uplands – e.g. Dolwyddelan, Dolbadarn, Carreg Cennen.

In the late 13th century, after fighting the Normans for 200 years, the armies of Gwynedd were defeated by Edward I who built a line of coastal castles and colonial towns as part of his efforts to conquer Wales. He nearly bankrupted his kingdom with his lavish building scheme. A century later, these castles were isolated and inefficient when Owain Glyndŵr's revolt swept through the land in the longest rebellion in the history of the British empire.

The castles, although part of the land, bear a deeper meaning as a reminder of being an oppressed nation, suffering numerous enemy invasions. But nowadays, they are also a source of pride – we were such a resilient and unconquerable nation!

(from top, left to right)
Castell Caerffili, **Caerphilly castle**
Castell Aberystwyth, **Aberystwyth castle**
Castell Harlech, **Harlech castle**

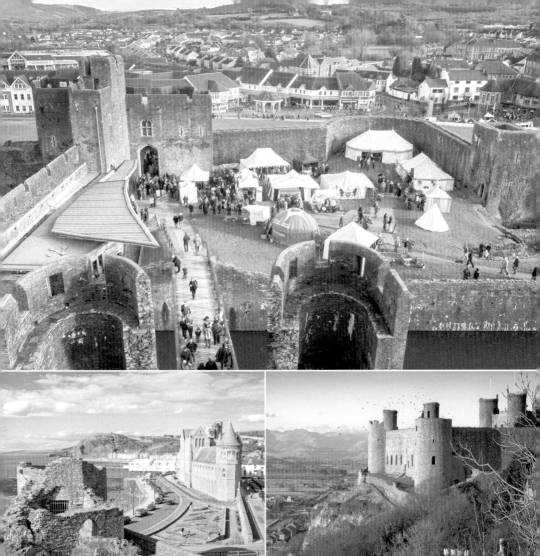

Amgueddfa Werin Cymru Sain Ffagan, Caerdydd
St Fagan National Museum of History, Cardiff

Sain Ffagan was established in 1948. It's an open-air museum that boasts many different historic buildings, from farmhouses to workshops, all representing Welsh culture and heritage at specific periods in history.

Amgueddfa Genedlaethol y Glannau, Abertawe
National Waterfront Museum, Swansea

This museum opened its doors in 2005. It combines maritime, transport and technology and is located in the Marina in Abertawe.

Amgueddfa Lechi Cymru, Llanberis   National Slate Museum, Llanberis

At the National Slate Museum, slate dressing, quarrymen's cottages and a bilingual film can be seen.

Llyfrgell Genedlaethol Cymru, Aberystwyth
National Library of Wales, Aberystwyth

The National Library offers reading rooms, exhibitions and events. Not only does it store every book published in Britain, it also houses the most precious books in Welsh history.

Big Pit Amgueddfa Lofaol Cymru, Blaenafon   Big Pit National Coal Museum

The Big Pit experience in Blaenafon offers the opportunity to visit the mines and learn more about the Welsh industrial mining heritage. It was a working coal mine from 1880 to 1980 and was opened to the public in 1983.

(from top, left to right)
Big Pit National mining museum
National Museum Cardiff
Maritime museum at Nefyn

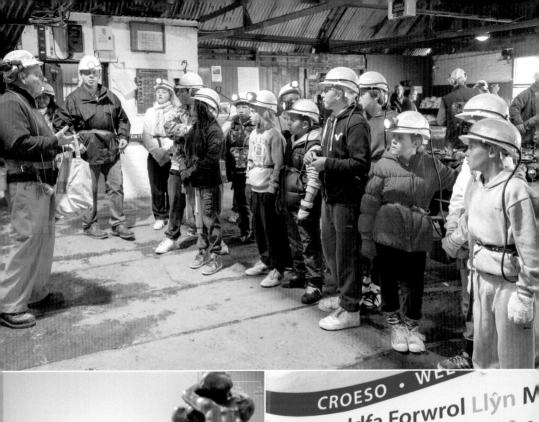

Gardd Garden

Gardd Fotaneg Genedlaethol Cymru
National Botanic Garden of Wales

The Botanic Garden of Wales located in Llanarthne, Carmarthenshire was opened in 2000 and boasts an amazing collection of over 8000 different plant varieties, spread across 560 acres of countryside. They also have the world's largest single-spanned glasshouse, designed by Lord Foster.

Gardd Bodnant Garden

Spread over 80 acres of land in the Conwy Valley, Bodnant Garden is world famous.

Bodnant (a dwelling by a stream) dates back to the mid-1700s when a mansion was built to replace an earlier house and parkland developed around Bodnant Hall. Today, Bodnant is owned and run by the National Trust.

Gerddi Aberglasne Gardens

Aberglasne consists of a mansion, an art gallery and gardens. The house and gardens were vandalised and neglected until 1995 when they were bought by Aberglasne Restoration Trust. The ground reopened to the public in 1999.

Gerddi Glan Hafren
Glansevern Hall Gardens

near Welshpool (Y Trallwng) SY21 8AH

Romantically positioned on the banks of the river Severn with gardens that extend to more than 25 acres. By 1982, the estate and hall had fallen into dereliction, and the Thomases worked incredibly hard over many years to restore it to a fully functioning estate. Their work in the gardens was particularly prolific, and so it was that they came to open their gardens up to the public in 1996.

Pyllau Lili, Bosherston, Sir Benfro
Lilly Ponds, Bosherston, Pembrokeshire

The Lily Ponds is a National Trust site walking trail that's famous for its waterlilies and otters. It's classed as an easy mile long walk and dog-friendly. It also offers the option to explore the dunes and pools of the Mere Pool Valley behind Broadhaven beach.

★ What's to see? – National Parks

Parc Cenedlaethol Eryri   **Snowdonia National Park**
Formed in 1951, Snowdonia National Park was the first **Parc Cenedlaethol** in Cymru. Parc Cenedlaethol Eryri is also the biggest in Wales as it covers 823 square miles. The National Park is also home to Yr Wyddfa (Snowdon) the highest mountain in Wales.

Parc Cenedlaethol Bannau Brycheiniog   **Brecon Beacons National Park**
Formed in 1957, the Brecon Beacons National Park covers 519 square miles. The whole of the National Park has been designated an International Dark Sky Reserve since 2013, which makes it the best place to gaze at the stars.

Parc Cenedlaethol Arfordir Penfro   **Pembrokeshire Coast National Park**
Formed in 1952, Pembrokeshire Coast National Park has a spectacular coastline and covers 243 square miles. Parc Cenedlaethol Arfordir Penfro is Britain's only coastal park and it's clear to see why when you visit its beautiful coastline.

(from top, left to right)
Snowdonia National Park
Brecon Beacons National Park
Cwm Abergwaun in the Pembrokeshire Coast National Park

PARC CENEDLAETHOL ERYRI

SNOWDONIA
NATIONAL PARK

PARC CENEDLAETHOL BANNAU BRYCHEINIOG

**Eisteddfod Genedlaethol Cymru
The National Eisteddfod of Wales**

The Eisteddfod is a festival to celebrate the talents of Wales. It changes location each year, alternating between north and south. There are literary, singing, reciting and dancing competitions in the main pavilion and a variety of stalls around the festival field. The Eisteddfod is held for eight days during the summer and is a great place to visit to get a real feel for the Welsh language, heritage and culture.

Things to look out for
Maes D the place to be if you're at any stage of your journey as a new Welsh speaker

Try these
Lle mae'r maes?
Where's the Eisteddfod field?
Lle mae'r maes parcio?
Where's the car park?
Lle mae Maes D? **where's Maes D?**

Lle mae'r bar gwyrdd?
Where's the green bar?
Lle mae'r pafiliwn?
Where's the pavilion?

Pryd mae'r Cadeirio?
When's the chairing ceremony?
Pryd mae'r Coroni?
When's the crowning ceremony?
Pryd mae cystadleuaeth medal y dysgwyr?
When's the learner's medal competition?
Pryd mae'r gig? **When's the gig?**

You might hear
Mae'r Coroni dydd Llun
The crowning ceremony is on Monday
Mae'r Cadeirio dydd Gwener
The chairing ceremony is on Friday
Mae medal y dysgwyr dydd Mercher
The learner's competition is on Wednesday
Mae'r gig heno! **The gig's on tonight!**

★ Events 2 – Food Festivals

Gŵyl Fwyd
Food Festival

Just as other countries celebrate their food, we do the same in Wales! There are many food festivals scattered all across Wales. If you visit one, why not try to ask for something yn Gymraeg?

A simple naming of what you want and adding **os gwelwch yn dda** is acceptable, exactly the same as you would do in English: **peint, os gwelwch yn dda**

| **Dw i'n** | **figan** | **vegan** |
| **I'm a** | **llysieuwr** | **vegetarian** |

Dw i ddim yn bwyta	**cnau**	**nuts**
I don't eat	**bwyd môr**	**sea food**
	bwyd glwten	**gluten**
	porc	**pork**
	gwenith	**wheat**
	bwyd poeth	**spicy food**

★ Events 2 – Food Festivals again!

Traditionally **medd (mead)** was used to welcome guests and ensure their loyalty. A medieval Welsh poem called 'Y Gododdin' recites how the Brythonic leader, Mynyddog Mwynfawr, gathered 300 Brythonic warriors and fed them mead for a whole year before going to battle so that they would pledge allegiance and thank him with loyalty. Drinking **cwrw (beer)** in Wales doesn't contractually oblige allegiance to the country, but once you get a taste for the great beers and ales produced here, you'll want to try them again and again!

cwrw	**beer**
gwin	**wine**
gwin gwyn	**white wine**
gwin coch	**red wine**
gwin rhosliw	**rosé wine**
wisgi	**whiskey**
peint	**a pint**
potel	**a bottle**
Iechyd da!	**Good health! / Cheers!**

Farming is an important industry in **Cymru** and **Cig Oen Cymru (Welsh Lamb)** and **Cig Eidion Cymru (Welsh Beef)** have achieved the prestigious Protected Geographical Indication (PGI) awarded by the European Commission, which means that the produce is protected and considered a speciality with connection to the land it comes from.

Sioe Fawr Llanelwedd
Royal Welsh Agricultural Show

Sioe Fawr Llanelwedd or the Royal Welsh is a four-day agricultural event at the showground in Llanelwedd near Builth Wells. Although there are many smaller, local agricultural shows in and around Wales, the Royal Welsh is the biggest.

Can't find them, ask
Lle mae'r anifeiliad?
Where are the animals?
Ble mae'r cneifio?
Where is the shearing?
Lle mae'r crefftau?
Where are the crafts?

Animals

defaid	**sheep**
gwartheg	**cows**
moch	**pigs**
ceffylau	**horses**
adar	**birds**
ieir	**hens**
ceiliogod	**cockerels**
cwningod	**rabbits**

Have seen them, say
Dw i wedi gweld y crefftau
I have seen the crafts
Dw i wedi gweld y cneifio
I have seen the shearing
Dw i wedi gweld y moch
I have seen the pigs

Want to know when, ask
Pryd mae'r cneifio?

Competitions

cneifio	**shearing**
trafod gwlân	**wool handling**
crefftau	**crafts**
cwympo coed	**tree felling**
torri coed	**wood chopping**
tynnu rhaff	**tug-of-war**

When's the shearing?
Pryd mae'r tynnu rhaff?
When's the tug-of-war?
Pryd mae'r torri coed?
When's the wood chopping?

★ Events 4 – Sports for all

Whatever sport you're into, there is a variety of sporting events around Wales.

Rally GB
Iron Man Wales, Pembrokeshire
Speedway Grand Prix at the
Principality Stadium
Welsh National Surfing
Championships, Pembrokeshire
Welsh Optimist Championship

There are various of opportunities to experience the beautiful landscapes and seascapes of Wales if you're a keen runner. Why not try
Hanner Marathon Caerdydd
Cardiff Half Marathon
Marathon Cymru, Llanelli
Wales Marathon, Llanelli
Marathon Eryri Snowdonia Marathon
Ras yr Wyddfa Snowdon Race

If you prefer a cycling competition, why not try
Velothon Wales
Tour de Môn, Anglesey
Snowdonia Etape

If you're not so keen on competitions and would like a more leisurely cycle, Wales has a national cycling route called **Lôn Las Cymru (the Welsh green* lane)** that runs from Caergybi (Holyhead) to Caerdydd (Cardiff) or Cas-gwent (Chepstow). The route is 250 miles long and is a fantastic opportunity to experience tourist sites, natural attractions and castles such as, Plas Newydd, Ynys Môn; Llyn Clywedog; Centre for Alternative Technology, Machynlleth; Elan Valley, Brecon Cathedral; Cardiff Castle and Cardiff Bay.

***glas (blue)** is sometimes used for green in Welsh, as in '**glaswellt**' **(grass)**.

★ Natural World 1 – Mountains

Mynyddoedd Cymru
The Welsh Mountains

The three highest peaks in Wales are Yr Wyddfa (1,085m), Cader Idris (893m) and Pen-y-Fan (886m).

Snowdon literally means 'snow(e)d on' or 'snow hill', but the Welsh **Yr Wyddfa** has so much more history and magic to its name. Yr Wyddfa derives from Gwyddfa which means tumulus, a mound of earth raised over a grave. Legend has it that when the giant Rhita Gawr was defeated by King Arthur and buried, so many people came to visit the site with stones or rocks to place on top of him that the tumulus grew and grew until we have what we today call Yr Wyddfa, the highest peak in Wales!

golygfa / golygfeydd	view(s)
mynydd(oedd)	mountain(s)
llwybr(au)	path(s)
copa	summit
carnedd(au)	cairn(s)
map	map
esgidau cerdded	hiking boots

You might see or hear
gofalus!   **careful!**
mae'r llwybr yn llithrig
the path is slippery
mae'r llwybr yn serth
the path is steep
mae'r olygfa yn fendigedig
the view is marvellous
mae'r copa yn bell
the summit is far

Try asking
Tryfan ydy'r mynydd yma?
Is this Tryfan?
Cader Idris ydy'r mynydd yma?
Is this Cader Idris?
Yr Wyddfa ydy'r mynydd yma?
Is this Snowdon?

You might hear

Ie	**Yes**
Nage	**No**

★ Natural World 2 – Coastline

The coastal path stretches over 870 miles and passes through two National Parks, Snowdonia and Pembrokeshire, and three Areas of Outstanding Natural Beauty (AONB), Ynys Môn (Anglesey), Llŷn and Gŵyr (Gower).

Llwybr Arfordir Cymru
Wales Coast Path

Things you might see along the way…

ynys(oedd)	**island(s)**
craig / creigiau	**rock(s)**
goleudy	**lighthouse**
traeth(au)	**beach(es)**
môr	**sea**
ton(nau)	**wave(s)**
cwch / cychod	**boat(s)**
llong(au)	**ship(s)**
morlo(i)	**seal(s)**

Cantre'r Gwaelod
The Sunken Hundred
Legend has it that there was a dry stretch of land between **Aberteifi (Cardigan)** and **Ynys Enlli (Bardsey Island)** and that this land was called **Gwlad Gwyddno (Gwyddno's Country)**. Gwyddno was the king of this land. To keep the sea at bay there was a great sea-wall with floodgates. One evening, Gwyddno threw a party for everyone in the land, except Seithenyn, who was left in charge of the floodgates. It was a stormy night and Seithenyn decided to leave his post and join everyone else inside to drink some mead. Of course, he drank too much and forgot about the floodgates and slowly the sea started to work its way into the kingdom. Everyone drowned, except Gwyddno. When there's a low tide, especially in Borth, near Aberystwyth, tree stumps and roots become visible and some think that these are the remains of Gwlad Gwyddno, or Cantre'r Gwaelod.

*Sunset Machlud **Cardiff Bay** Bae Caerdydd*

Llyn Tegid, y Bala
Y llyn naturiol mwyaf yng Nghymru.

Llyn Tegid, Bala
The largest natural lake in Wales.

Afon Tywi
Yr afon hiraf yng Nghymru.

River Tywi
The longest river in Wales is Afon Tywi.

Traphont Ddŵr Pontcysyllte, Llangollen
Un o dri safle treftadaeth byd yng Nghymru
One of three world heritage sites in Wales

Pontcysyllte Aqueduct Llangollen

Afon Dyfrdwy	**River Dee**	Llyn Celyn
Afon Gwy	**River Wye**	Llyn y Gadair
Afon Tawe	**River Tawe**	Llyn Llydaw
Afon Ystwyth	**River Ystwyth**	Llyn Ogwen
Afon Menai	**Menai Strait**	Llyn Clywedog
Afon Hafren	**River Severn**	Llyn Efyrnwy

camlas **canal**

Camlas Trefaldwyn (Montgomery)
Camlas Aberdâr
Camlas Sir Fynwy a Brycheiniog
(Monmouth and Brecon)
Camlas Castell-nedd (Neath)
Camlas Abertawe (Swansea)
Camlas Morgannwg (Glamorgan)

★ Natural World 4 – Woodlands

When you think of Welsh woodland, you wouldn't necessarily think of a rainforest, would you? Interestingly enough, Britain does have a few rainforests in Cumbria, Scotland, England and north Wales! If you visit Snowdonia, make sure you take a stroll through Coed Llennyrch and Coed Felinrhyd, Maentwrog, to experience the rainforest for yourself!

Pa adar sy 'ma?
What (breed of) birds are here?

You might hear
Mae 'na ... yma
There are ... here

coed	wood
coeden	a tree
coedwig	woodland
coedwigoedd	woodlands
deilen	a leaf
dail	leaves
mainc	bench
blodau	flowers
clychau'r gog	bluebells
garlleg gwyllt	wild garlic
aderyn	a bird
adar	birds

coed sycamor	sycamore trees
coed derw	oak trees
coed helyg	willow trees
coed ffawydd	beech trees
coed celyn	holly trees
coed pîn	pine
coed ynn	ash trees
cwcw	cuckoo
siffsaff	chiffchaff
cnocell y coed	woodpecker
tylluan	owl
gwalch y pysgod	osprey
eryr	eagle
barcud coch	red kite

Ask
Pa goed sy 'ma?
What (type of) trees are here?

★ Activities 1 – At the seaside

traeth	beach	Gweithgareddau / Activities
glan y môr	seaside	
haul	sun	pysgota — **to fish**
gwylan	seagull	caiacio / ceufadio — **to kayak**
môr	sea	canŵio — **to canoe**
ton	wave	padlfyrddio — **to paddle-board**
tonnau	waves	syrffio — **to surf**
tywod	sand	nofio — **to swim**
cwch	boat	deifio — **to dive**
cragen / cregyn	seashells	snorclio — **to snorkle**
goleudy	lighthouse	
fflagiau / baneri	flags	Try
pêl	a ball	**Ar lan y môr dw i'n licio nofio.**
barcud	kite	**At the seaside I like to swim.**
castell tywod	sandcastle	**Ar lan y môr dw i'n hoffi syrffio.**
bwced a rhaw	bucket and spade	**At the seaside I like to surf.**
hufen iâ	ice cream	**Ar lan y môr dw i'n licio pysgota.**
eli haul	suncream	**At the seaside I like to fish.**
tywel	towel	**Ar lan y môr dw i'n hoffi ymlacio.**
sbectol haul	sunglasses	**At the seaside I like to relax.**

Ask
Lle mae'r traeth? Where's the beach?
Ble mae'r eli haul?
Where's the suncream?
Lle mae'r ymbarél?
Where's the umbrella?

pysgota	to fish	hwyaden	duck
pysgota plu	fly-fishing	alarch	swan
pysgota	coarse-fishing	crëyr glas	heron
gwialen bysgota	a fishing rod	glas y dorlan	kingfisher
rhwyd	a net	hwyaid	ducks
trwydded bysgota	fishing license	elyrch	swans
		gŵydd	a goose
pysgod	fish (p.)	gwyddau	goose (p.)
pysgodyn	a fish	pioden y môr	oyster catcher
brithyll	trout	bilidowcar	cormorant
brithyll seithliw	rainbow trout		
carp	carp	Dw i wedi gweld glas y dorlan	
penhwyad	pike	I've seen a kingfisher	
llysywen	eel	Dw i wedi dal pysgodyn	
penbwl	tadpole	I've caught a fish	
llyffant	frog / toad		
broga	frog		

★ Activities 3 – On the Rocks

Cymru has a rich industrial past, from the south Wales mines to the quarries in the north. During the eighteenth and nineteenth centuries, Wales led the work on the industrial front, using its natural resources, slate, copper, iron, coal and timber, to its advantage. This came to a halt in the 1970s–80s when mines and quarries were closed and workers made redundant.

But Wales' industrial history has been brought to life in the form of museums and hands-on experiences such as The Big Pit experience in Blaenafon where you can visit the mines and learn more about Welsh mining history. The Llechwedd Slate Caverns in Blaenau Ffestiniog let you explore deep underground caverns and go on an off-road adventure above ground.

If you're not interested in learning more about the history of mining and the quarries in Wales and want to enjoy something a bit different then look no further than Zip World. They offer unique adventures in the heart of Snowdonia National Park where you can be part of Wales's unique heritage deep in the slate quarry or up high with a brilliant birds-eye view of the landscape.

Try
Dw i eisiau mynd ar y Zip Wire os gwelwch yn dda
I want to go on the Zip Wire please
Dw i eisiau mynd i Bounce Below os gwelwch yn dda
I want to go to Bounce Below please

★ Activities 4 – On your bike!

Many of Wales' cycle trails follow the remains of its industrial path, tramways and old railway lines where you can cycle traffic-free and appreciate the beautiful scenery from golden beaches to mountain ranges. In addition to the **Lôn Las**, the cycle trail that runs from one end of the country to the other, there are other (shorter) routes that might appeal…

Lôn Eifion is a 12.5 mile cycle route from Bryncir to Caernarfon, or Eifionydd to Arfon.

Llwybr Beicio – Rheidol – Cycle Trail
An 11 mile trail from Aberystwyth to Cwm Rheidiol where you will be able to visit the famous Pontarfynach or Devil's Bridge, a place of Outstanding Natural Beauty. Legend has it that the Devil offered to help an old lady retrieve her cow from the other side of the river by building a bridge for her and all he wanted in return was the first thing that crossed the bridge. The old lady returned the following morning with her dog and was greeted by the Devil and his bridge and his request to keep her side of the bargain. She threw a loaf of bread over to the other side of the bridge and her dog ran to fetch it. The Devil was outwitted and was never to be seen in Wales again!

Llwybr Arfordirol y Mileniwm – Llanelli – Millennium Coastal Path
Is a 10.5 mile cycle route from Bynea to Pen-bre (Pembrey).

beic	bike
beicio	to bike / to cycle
llwybr	trail
llwybr beicio	cycle route / trail
llwybrau beicio	cycle routes / trails

Dw i'n licio beicio	I like to cycle
Mae'n fendigedig yma	It's marvellous here
Mae'r olygfa yn hyfryd	The view is delightful
Mae'r llwybr beicio yma'n grêt	This cycle route is great

There are many routes and paths to choose from when walking in Wales, but the three most well-known are **Llwybr Arfordir Cymru (Wales Coast Path)** that stretches over 870 miles, **Llwybr Clawdd Offa (Offa's Dyke Path)** that follows the English-Welsh border, a total of 177 miles, and **Llwybr Llechi Eryri (Snowdonia Slate Trail)**, an 83-mile circular trail through Eryri.

You might see signs on your travels…

llwybr	**path / footpath**
llwybr cyhoeddus	**public footpath**
cylchdaith	**circular route**
map	**map**
rydych chi yma	**you are here**
dim mynediad	**no entry**
tir preifat	**private land**
camfa	**stile**
giât mochyn	**kissing gate**
afon	**river**
nant	**stream**
rheadr	**waterfall**
pont	**bridge**

Pa mor uchel ydy'r mynydd?
How high is the mountain?
Pa mor bell ydy'r daith gerdded?
How far is the walk?
Pa mor saff ydy'r llwybr?
How safe is the path?

It is not compulsory for businesses in Wales to display bilingual signs; more often than not it is a choice, a conscious decision. After years of protesting for the right to speak and use Welsh it now seems that the language is classed as a unique selling point for businesses, something that gives them that edge, and a one-up on the competition. Have a look at these signs; can you spot similar signs where you are?

Mon - Sat; 2 hours
No return
within 2 hours

Fish and Chips

Gifts

Butcher

Chemist

Barber

Books

ORIEL
Y MÔR

Galerie de
la mer

Sea
Gallery

Oriel Gallery

Cerddoriaeth

Music

Y POPTY

Bakehouse

Brewery

Hair salon

Post office

Ladies' clothes; Ladies' shoes

Fruits

Food; Drink; Entertainment

Beauty

Photo Shop

Police

Award-winning Ice Cream

Wine

Fish

Food and Drink

A simple naming of what you want and adding a plîs / os gwelwch yn dda is acceptable, exactly the same as you would do in English:

> **coffi, plîs.**
>
> **coffi, os gwelwch yn dda.**

Diodydd   Beverages

Welsh	English	Welsh	English
dŵr	water	fodca	vodka
dŵr pefriog / pigog	sparkling water	jin a tonic	gin and tonic
llefrith / llaeth	milk	wisgi	whiskey
sudd oren	orange juice		
sudd afal	apple juice	ysgafn	light
lemonêd	lemonade	tywyll	dark
panad	cuppa	potel	bottle
te	tea	peint	pint
coffi	coffee	gwydriad	glass
siocled poeth	hot chocolate		
te gwyrdd	green tea	sych	dry
		gwin y tŷ	house wine
cwrw	beer	melys	sweet
gwin	wine		
gwin gwyn	white wine		
gwin coch	red wine		
gwin rhosliw	rosé wine		

Ffrwythau a llysiau
Fruits and vegetables

afal	apple
banana	banana
oren	orange
mafon	raspberries
pinafal	pinapple
mefus	strawberries
ceirios	cherries
mango	mango
melon	melon
eirin	plums
letys	lettuce
ciwcymbar	cucumber
tomato	tomato
seleri	celery
pupur coch	red pepper
tatws	potatoes
moron	carrots
brocoli	broccoli
pys	peas
madarch	mushrooms
pannas	parsnips
cennin	leeks
riwbob	rhubarb
nionyn / winwns	onion

Cig a physgod
Meats and fish

cig oen	lamb
cig eidion	beef
cyw iâr	chicken
stecen	steak
bacwn / cig moch	bacon
sosej / selsig	sausage
hwyaden	duck
eog / samwn	salmon
penfras	cod
cimwch	lobster
corgimwch	prawn
macrell	mackerel
cregyn gleision	mussels
cranc	crab
sardîns	sardines
lleden fôr	plaice
tiwna	tuna

Llestri, pwdinau a chawsiau
Crockery, puddings and cheese

halen	salt	cawsiau	cheeses
pupur	pepper	caws coch	Llŷn red cheese
olew	oil	caws cry	strong cheese
finag / finegr	vinegar	caws gafr	goat's cheese
potel	bottle	caws Cymreig	Welsh cheese
gwydr	glass	caws Caerffili	Caerphilly cheese
fforc	fork	caws Caer	Cheshire cheese
cyllell	knife		
llwy	spoon		
plât	plate		
powlen	bowl		

pwdin bara menyn	bread and butter pudding
pwdin reis	rice pudding
pwdin taffi	sticky toffee pudding
crymbl riwbob	rhubarb crumble
crymbl afal	apple crumble
tarten ffrwythau	fruit tart
salad ffrwythau	fruit salad
hufen iâ	ice cream
hufen	cream
cwstard	custard

A plate of Welsh cheeses

Amser brecwast
Breakfast time

uwd	porridge	crempog	pancake
grawnfwyd	cereal	crempogau	pancakes
tôst	toast	ffrwyth	a fruit
bara	bread	ffrwythau	fruit
jam	jam	iogwrt	yoghurt
mêl	honey	brecwast llawn	full Welsh
menyn	butter	cocos	cockles
		bara lawr	laver bread
wy	egg	madarch	mushrooms
wyau	eggs	pwdin gwaed	black pudding
wyau wedi'u sgramblo	scrambled eggs	cig moch	bacon
wy wedi'i ferwi	boiled egg	sbigoglys	spinach
wy wedi'i ffrio	fried egg	ffa pob	baked beans
wy wedi'i botsio	poached egg		

The National Anthem

Yr Anthem Genedlaethol:
Hen Wlad fy Nhadau

Mae hen wlad fy nhadau yn annwyl i mi
gwlad beirdd a chantorion, enwogion o fri
ei gwrol ryfelwyr, gwladgarwyr tra mad,
dros ryddid collasant eu gwaed.

Gwlad, gwlad,
pleidiol wyf i'm gwlad
tra môr yn fur
i'r bur hoff bau
o bydded i'r heniaith barhau

The National Anthem:
Land of my Fathers

The land of my fathers is dear to me
land of poets and singers, famous people of
renown
her brave warriors, very good patriots
for freedom they lost their blood

Country, Country (Wales, Wales)
I'm faithful to my Country
While the sea is a wall
to the dear pure Country
Oh may (our) old language endure

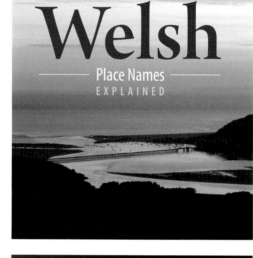
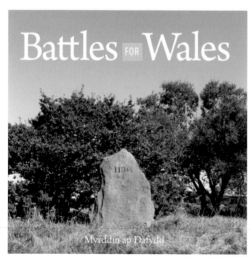
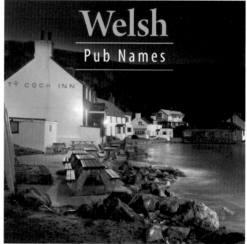

Welsh Poetry
in translation

Howard Huws

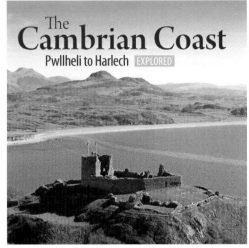

The
Cambrian Coast
Pwllheli to Harlech EXPLORED

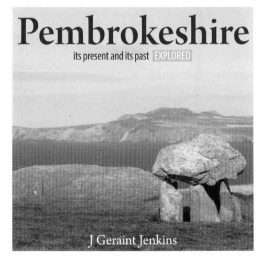

Pembrokeshire
its present and its past EXPLORED

J Geraint Jenkins

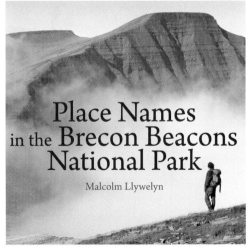

Place Names
in the Brecon Beacons
National Park

Malcolm Llywelyn

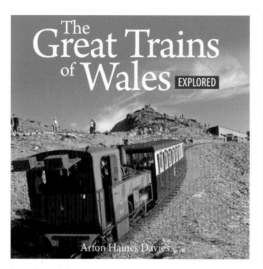

The Great Trains of Wales EXPLORED

Arfon Haines Davies

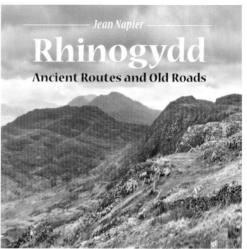

Jean Napier

Rhinogydd

Ancient Routes and Old Roads

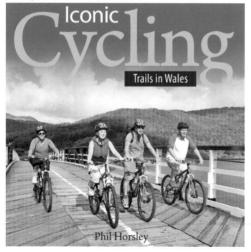

Iconic Cycling

Trails in Wales

Phil Horsley

The Shepherd War Poet

Hedd Wyn
(Ellis H. Evans 1887-1917)
introduction by Gruffudd Antur

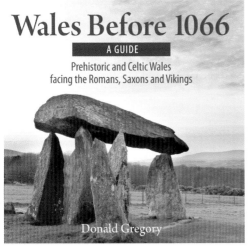

Wales Before 1066

A GUIDE

Prehistoric and Celtic Wales
facing the Romans, Saxons and Vikings

Donald Gregory

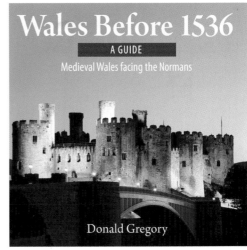

Wales Before 1536

A GUIDE

Medieval Wales facing the Normans

Donald Gregory

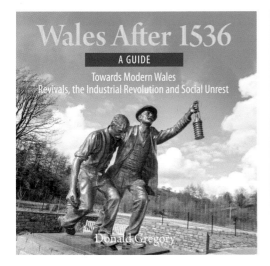

Wales After 1536

A GUIDE

Towards Modern Wales
Revivals, the Industrial Revolution and Social Unrest

Donald Gregory

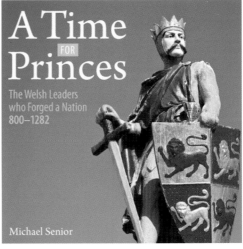

A Time FOR Princes

The Welsh Leaders
who Forged a Nation
800–1282

Michael Senior

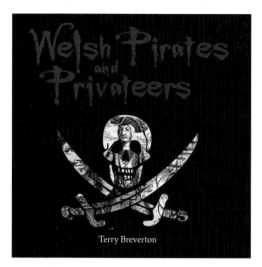

Welsh Pirates and Privateers

Terry Breverton

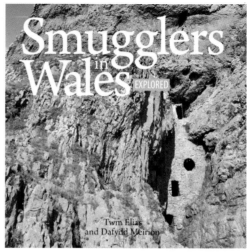

Smugglers in Wales EXPLORED

Twm Elias and Dafydd Meirion

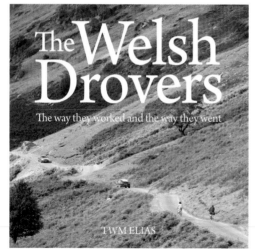

The Welsh Drovers

The way they worked and the way they went

TWM ELIAS

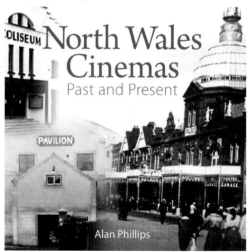

North Wales Cinemas
Past and Present

Alan Phillips